Written by David Thomas Illustrated by Angela Thorp

POTTY POEMS

First published in Great Britain in 2016 by
Alphabet School Books Limited
21 Pear Tree Close, Hadfield, Glossop, Derbyshire SK13 2HA,
England

A CIP catalogue record for this book
is available from The British Library

ISBN
978-0-9926324-1-0

Printed by Bell and Bain Limited
in the United Kingdom

Contents

Pretty Little Tree
Mucky Maurice
Trumping Great Gran
Simon Slugbreath's Cat
Mr Turner and the Bunsen Burner
Lucky Lucy Locket
Mary's Plot
Re-cycling
Peter Jackson's Friend
Don't Look Up

Marvin the Magician

Marvin the magician was all the rage,
A nine year old superstar walked on stage.
He strolled about with a magic wand in his hand,
The music was loud, from the theatre's large band,

He shouted I am going to pull out a rabbit from this top hat,
But when he pulled out his hand it was a large ginger cat.

His magic wand was ready and able,
But that snapped in half when he tapped the table.
"Oh no," he sighed the audience will think I am thick,
I really must pull off a fantastic trick.

Some of the audience laughed thinking he was a fool,
Some even booed which seemed rather cruel.
Marvin glared at the crowd with a smile on his face,
He knew very soon he'd be leaving this place.

There was a loud whoosh that everyone heard,
Then a big puff of smoke and he'd disappeared.

Nazeem Joins The Circus

Nazeem joined the travelling circus
He thought he'd be a clown
Nazeem was the unfuniest person
That had ever been to town

He thought he would try his hand
At being an acrobat

He spun three and a half times
Instead of four
And landed on his back

Next he tried the high wire
But his balance was very very poor

He wobbled seventeen times
Before he hit the floor

Nazeem rose to his feet
Shouting, "I will not be done"

I'm going to be a lion tamer
And I will be number one

He put his head in the lions mouth
He could hear the loud applause

The lion thought enough is enough
And closed his great big jaws.

Jim the Gymnast

Little Jim Shaw is pretty cool,
He runs three miles every day to school.

As the school bell rings at the end of the day
There is just a blur as Jim speeds away.

Another three miles was easy peasy
But he knew his dream would never be easy.

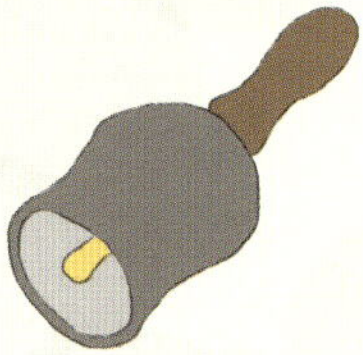

Arriving home he vaulted the gate
Just in time (he's never late.)

When his mother opened the front door
Jim did a roly poly onto the floor,

Followed by a somersault over the settee
Landing on his chair just in time for tea.

His mother sighed and then she gasped
As Jim said "I'm going to be the world's best gymnast!"

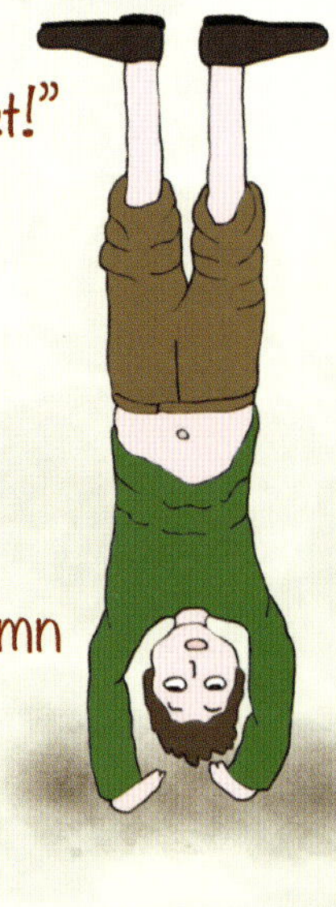

Monday morning he was late for school
He meant to be late - he wasn't a fool.

A quick handstand and he was over the gate,
A teacher shouted "Jim Shaw! You. Are. Late!"

The entire school was in the hall, singing a hymn
But nothing could stop Gymnast Jim.

He shot up the curtains like a snake up a tree.
Here we go! He counted "One, two three!"

He leapt off the curtain rail and headed to the ground,
The whole room fell silent, there wasn't a sound.

As Jim's fingertips touched the floor,
He rolled four times to a fantastic roar.

Another three rolls before he leapt in the air,
Spinning three times without a care.

He landed on his feet in the centre of the stage
The Head fainted - she's at a funny old age.

The crowd looked on, all of them aghast.
"Morning all! I'm Jim the Gymnast!"

Grandad

Sally Worsnip Beckitt's Grandad was a funny old chap.
He wore a thick woolly scarf and a tatty old flat cap.

He took some snuff from an old tin sniffed it up his nose.
"Eeeh," he shouted, "that's shifted my bogeys and my crows."

He burped on the bus and it was very, very loud
The bus was full of a chanting football crowd.

Leaving the bus he shouted,
"Come on the blues as he knew the football fans were reds."
They shouted naughty words and threw tomatoes at our heads.

Grandad was laughing loudly as we escaped into a large clothes shop.
When he lunged at a dummy modelling clothes and gave it a karate chop.

The dummies head fell off and rolled along the floor.
We had to run quickly as we were chased from the store.

Returning home Sally told her mother that Grandad had been bad.
Sally's mother glared at her and said, "I think it's pretty sad,
That you make up silly stories about your little old Grandad."

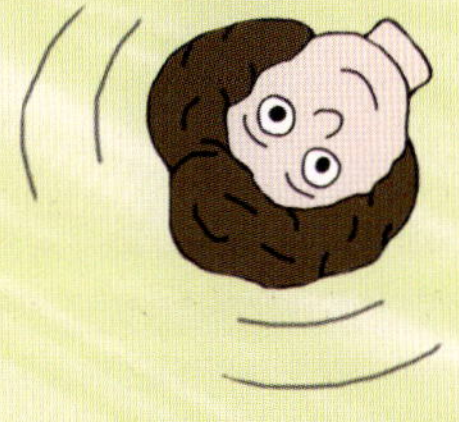

Rose's Nose

Rose has a big red spot on the end of her nose

Nobody knows,

Apart from Rose,

How Rose got the spot on the end of her nose

Do you know?

(Answer on page Six and a bit)

Our Little Mouse

A short while ago
A little mouse
Used to play about
In our little house

We put a little tray
On the floor
With scraps of food
Just near the old back door

But late one night he got greedy
And came back for more
But he'd forgotten
About the big ginger cat next door

He walked across the kitchen floor
Still wet from the rain
When the big ginger cat snapped his jaws
Our little mouse was never seen again.

Victor's Underpants

Victor the ice-cream man parks his van
At the entrance to the park,
He's there early in the morning
He's still there when it gets dark.

Children queue for ice-creams and lollies
Sometimes for crisps or a sweet,
Victor had them all in his van
Stacked up nice and neat.

Things were going really well
During a sunny spell in May,
When suddenly there was an explosion
What happened, who can say?

Some say Victor headed skywards
As he shot through the roof,
But as he's never been found
There isn't any proof.

Little Simon Cornet
Said he saw it all,
The day the ice-cream van blew up
Some bits even hit the wall.

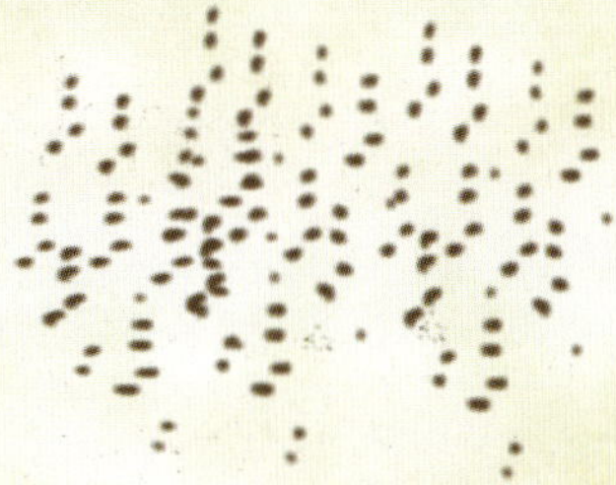

A large box of chopped nuts
Sailed through the air,
They sprinkled down like raindrops
Into everybody's hair.

Raspberry sauce splashed everywhere
Flakes and sprinkles landed on the old church roof,
But there was only Simon Cornet
Who had the truth and the proof.

Simon said he was eating a 99
Chilled out and relaxed,
When the elastic in Victor's underpants
Suddenly snapped.

Now Simon Cornet is not a reliable witness
As he is only three,
People said he could only say
What that day he did see.

Simon Cornet was questioned by his parents
The police plus his uncles and his aunt's,
But he was adamant the van blew up
When the elastic snapped in Victor's underpants.

Tommy Winston Boyd

My best mate Tommy is football mad,
When you talk about Chelsea he's never ever sad,
He has football posters on his bedroom wall,
But his pride and joy is his tresured Chelsea ball.

Tom's eyes lit up when he got a ticket for the game off Uncle Joe,
Suddenly he took ill ....Tommy couldn't go,
He wouldn't see the players turn out on the pitch,
So I wrote a letter to Chelsea's owner Roman Abramovich.

Tommy was ill for ages ....which didn't seem fair,
He lost his lovely smile ....and all of his hair,
They let me visit him at weekends in the afternoon,
I read him Chelsea's match reports to help lift his gloom.

Three months later and Tommy had survived,
When he came home from hospital a parcel had arrived,
Tommy's mother opened the parcel and screeched in a high pitch,
"It's from Chelsea's owner Roman Abramovich."
Inside were four tickets for a match in a private box
As well as a blue Chelsea shirt, shorts and socks.

Loud Sneeze

One bright autumn day I walked through an orchard
Full of apple trees
Suddenly a fly flew up my nose
I let out a great big sneeze
The earth shook
Followed by a very large sound
As all the apples fell off the trees
And landed on the ground.

Anne-Marie Plumstone

Anne-Marie Plumstone has a brother who can't write.
Poor Anne-Marie can't even sleep at night.

She feared for her brother as he cannot talk
And the poor little mite can't even walk.

She cried, "I don't even know why he has two feet
As he can't play football, with the boys on the street.

He cannot use a computer and he can't even sing,
I will get him sorted; I'll give the doctor a ring."

"Stop, stop, stop," shouted Mother so bold,
"Your poor little brother is only five days old."

Growing Up

Sally Slipknot tripped over
Because she didn't tie her laces.

Barry Brimstone's pants fell down
Because he didn't fasten his braces.

Lucy Lipstick banged her head
Because she was taller than the door.

Tommy Flintlock slipped on a banana skin
And landed on the floor.

Jack Trumper missed the bus
Because his watch was slow.

Alice Prune never watered her plant
And wondered why it didn't grow.

Lindsey sighed as she turned and glared at Ben
"Do you think when we grow up
We'll end up just as daft as them?"

Unfair

Gaia Rossi lives on our street
She wears big purple Doc Martens on her feet

Gaia always has a great big smile... especially for me
It's just so, so sad Gaia can"t see

Just seems so unfair... and so unkind
That my friend Gaia... was born blind.

The Bread Bin

Jack William Conn's Uncle Alex
Dropped the large heavy bread bin on his toe
Oh no!

Placing the really heavy lid back on the bread bin
Poor Uncle Alex trapped both of his thumbs
Oh crumbs!

Caz “Bonkers” Taylor

Caz Taylor loves leaving boys in a state of fright
She leaves them trembling by day and by night

She hides behind the curtains in the hall at school
Then leaps out at a boy howling like a ghost or a ghoul

One boy went to the toilet for a wee and a poo
But Caz had coated the seat with a dollop of super glue

He was stuck for an hour in a state of fright
Because Caz Taylor had turned out the light

She would not join in skipping or netball like the other girls do
Caz likes wrestling, karate and her favourite kung-fu

Caz Taylor had a trial for the school football team
She got picked......what a dream

But in her very first game she got a red card
For punching a player very very hard

Banned from all sports she didn't know what to do for the best
Then she saw a sign for the school conker contest

Caz smashed every other conker, she was very very good
Nobody knew her conker was carved from a piece of wood

Martin Jake Joseph Bolton wasn't a fool
At morning assembly he addressed the entire school

He shouted "That Caz Taylor is flippin BONKERS"
And she cheats at blummin 'CONKERS'."

A Cat, A Dog and A Frog

A cat and a dog lived with a frog.
The frog was called Froggie.
The dog was called Doggie.
What was the cat called?

....

(Answer, page 300 & thirty 3)

P
6 & A BIT
G
E

George's Spider

Charlotte's little brother, George,
Has a spider that can't build a web.

Every night the spider sleeps
On the end of George's bed.

George wakes up every morning
With a smile upon his face.

As his favourite little spider
Is still in the same old place.

George puts the spider on his hand
As he trots off to school.

Old ladies scream “Kill it, kill it,
You silly little fool!”

George laughs loudly as he shouts,
“No! He’s fantastic,

I got him in a Christmas cracker
He’s really made of plastic!”

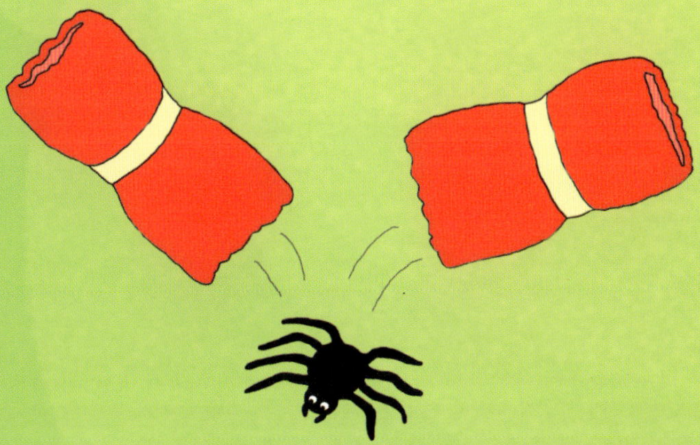

Heads, Shoulders, Knees and Toes

Jed banged his head
On the headboard of his bed.

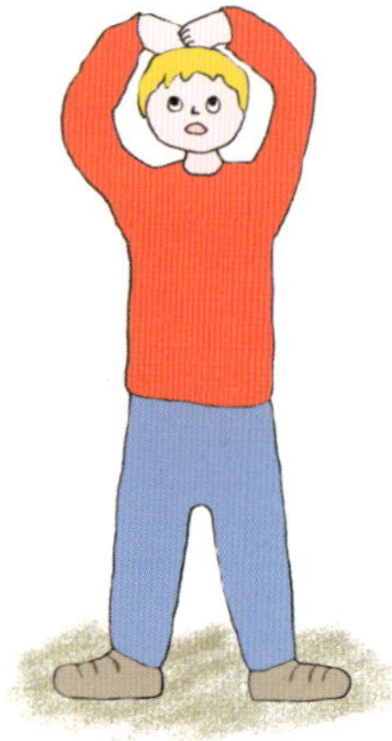

Bradley went climbing and cracked his shoulder
On a great big boulder.

Louise tripped over after a gigantic sneeze
The poor little mite scraped both of her knees.

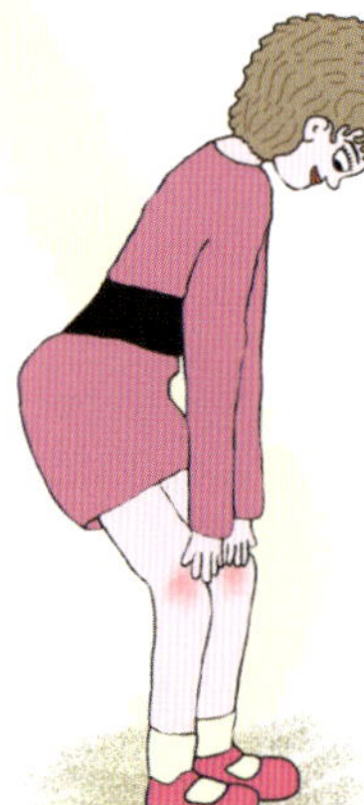

Poor little Rose
Dropped a plant pot on her toes.

Archie Turnip laughed out loud
Then bellowed like a football crowd.

What a bunch of fools,
They sing a song about you lot in primary schools.
(all together)

Heads, shoulders, knees and toes, knees and toes.

The Spy

Patrick Seamus Murphy claimed he was a spy,
Patrick strangely had one blue and one green eye,
He said he could see for thousands of miles with his green eye,
That's why he's a spy,
He wouldn't lie.

Molly, Dolly and Polly

Dolly and Polly are parrots,
They only eat diced carrots.
Molly is a girl who sings and shouts,
She only eats cabbage and brussels sprouts.

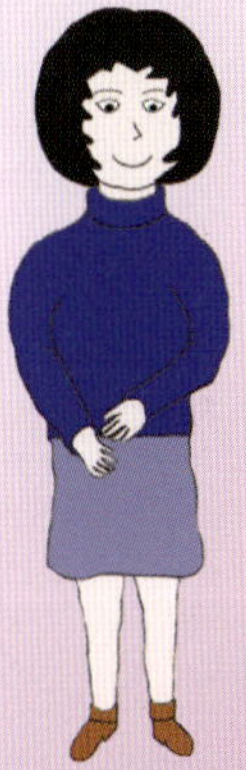

Mother worries about Molly,
Even though she's always jolly.
She also worries about the parrots,
But they seem happy eating carrots.

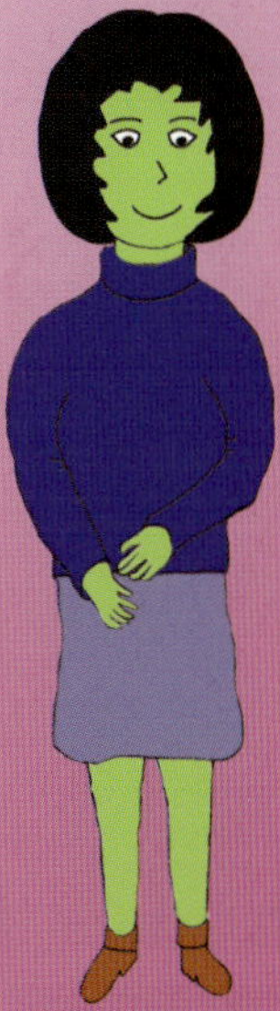

Then suddenly, one Sunday morning,
Mother collapsed from what she'd seen.
Polly and Dolly had turned bright orange
And Molly had turned a dark, shade of green!

The Zoo

Two monkeys at the local zoo
Found the keepers keys,
They knew what to do.

When the zoo closed at the end of the day,
It was time for the monkeys to have their way.
They opened some cages and let the birds fly up to the trees.
It's really good fun having a large bunch of keys.

Out came an elephant, a zebra and a gnu,
This was the monkey's idea of a proper zoo.
Penguins and sea lions leapt in to the children's paddling pool,
They splashed around in the water so cool.

Their keys opened the picnic food stall,
There were cakes and buns for all.
Once everything was greedily eaten with delight,
It was time to return to their homes for the night.

With all the animals locked up,
The keys were hidden away.
The keys would be used another day.

Jumping Jack

I'm Jumping Jack, I jump so high
I really want to reach the sky.

Clouds I see but what lies beyond?
I wish I had a magic wand.

I took my chance on a trampoline.
I went higher than I'd ever been.

Not high enough - in my mind's eye.
I really want to reach the sky.

I tried to be a human cannonball
The circus owner said I was too small.

Nobody knows my desire
To go beyond the cathedral spire.

Well I've got three pounds in my pocket -
I'm saving up to buy a rocket.

Tilly, Willy, Milly and Billy

Tilly, Willy, Milly and Billy
Really enjoyed being very silly,
Tilly and Milly started to sing
As Willy and Billy jumped on a swing,
They all laughed loudly
As they ran off that day,
When the park keeper chased them
Quickly away.

They entered a large shop
And tried on some clothes,
Why the boys wore dresses
Nobody knows,
They all laughed loudly
As they ran off that day,
As the shop assistant chased them
Quickly away.

All four of them thought
They could do as they like,
When they let down the tyres
On somebody's bike,
As the owner returned
They all ran away,
Giggling and shouting
"Hip, hip hooray."

They spotted a man
With no hair on his head.
"Cor blimey" said Willy
"That's perfect for an egg."
A free range egg sailed through the air
And landed on the head of the man with no hair,
They all laughed loudly as they sped away
Not knowing what was coming their way.

Turning the corner into a small cobbled street
They were confronted by a large pair of feet,
The policeman snarled; "Stand over there."
As they were joined by the man with no hair;
All four started crying and created a pool,
As the man with no hair
Was the head of their school.

Claudia

Claudia found a funny egg
When she returned to her nest.
The egg had lots of colours,
And was different from the rest.

Claudia glared at this strange egg
And looked down with a frown,
All of her usual eggs
Were always white or brown.

Claudia wondered, what kind of bird
Would leave an egg in her nest,
Knowing that she'd notice
It was different from the rest.

Tommy ran past Claudia,
Chased by his sister, Meg,
Screeching, "Tommy! Where have you hidden
My mini Easter egg?"

Auntie Charlotte's Budgie

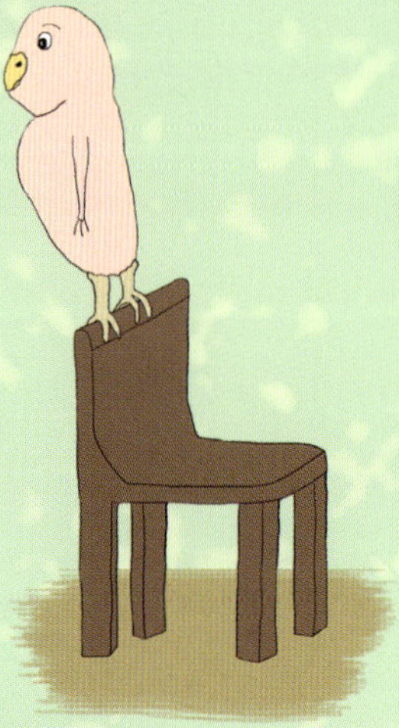

Auntie Charlotte's budgie has got no feathers
When he did they were a lovely shade of blue
Now he looks like a plucked chicken
Cock-a-doodle-doo.

My cousin Kyrstian goes to art school
He said "I know what to do"
I will buy a tin of gloss paint
And re-paint him a lovely shade of blue.

Kyrstian set to work and started painting budgie Polly
Who really wasn't feeling very jolly
He tried his best to fly away
Banged his head on the ceiling
Was not his lucky day.

Sadly the budgie headed towards the floor
Squawking cock-a-doodle-doo
Poor Polly created a splashing sound
As he landed in the paint pot tin of blue.

Now Polly's dead
No more cock-a-doodle-doo
We buried him in a wooden box
Painted in a lovely shade of blue.

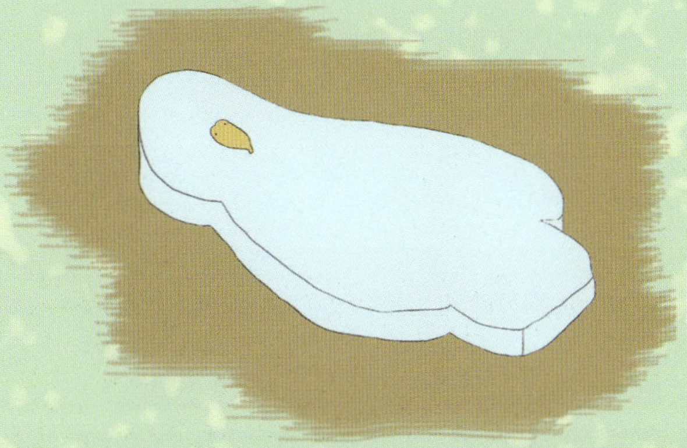

Page

300 & Thirty 3

ALBERT

Upside Down

This poem is upside down
Because I'm as daft as you

Don't try and deny it
You know, you know it's true

But I know a boy who's got it right
He worked it out in bed just the other night

He wears a cheesy grin
His name is Fred
He read this poem standing on his head.

Bogey and Snot

Our classroom teacher Mrs Crowsnott
Always has a bogey hanging from one side of her nose
As the day wears on I'm sure it grows and grows

Eventually it hangs down on a string of greyish green snot
If she turned her head sharply
Someone would cop the lot

Our headmaster Mr Trumpaminit
Burst through the classroom door
Mrs Crowsnott turned sharply
Bogey and snot were there no more

A bogey and string of snot hurtled through the air
All the kids ducked then laughed
As it landed in Mr Trumpaminits hair.

BUT

Stavros lives on High street
BUT
It was at the bottom of the town

Charlotte lives on Queen street
BUT
She doesn't have a crown

Jody went to Warmington
BUT
It was very very cold

Montserret bought a hot cross bun
BUT
It wasn't even warm

Toby is from the north
BUT
He supports Southend

Lucy walked down New street
BUT
The houses looked pretty old

Felix likes chicken wings
BUT
There's nothing wrong with his arms

Nigel eats Dundee cake
BUT
He's never been to Scotland

Tommy has athletes foot
BUT
He”s never run a race

Shabana went to Turkey
BUT
Doesn't like Christmas dinner

Now it's your turn
So don”t look down with a frown
See how many words you can find
That just might be upside down.

Making a Noise

Imogen the duck sunbathes lying on her back
Makes a noise that goes quack quack quack.

Ruben the horse in a field munches on a bale of hay
Creates a noise like neigh neigh neigh.

Carly the chicken lost her egg, that was bad luck
She made a noise cluck cluck cluck.

Barry the budgie has funny shaped feet
Squaking a noise tweet tweet tweet.

Leonardo the lion stood on a thorn and hurt his paw
He bellowed a noise like roar roar roar.

Tommy Nutbreath was sent to bed early
For throwing an apple pie
He made a noise like cry cry cry.

Apple Pie

Sally Mudflap was hit in the eye
By a large apple pie
That hurtled from the sky
My oh my it made her cry
That nasty apple pie
That came hurtling from the sky.

I'm Not Silly

My great grandma Gertrude called me a silly sausage
Which I thought wasn't very polite
But then I had second thoughts
My grandma Gertrude might just be right.

If a sausage wasn't silly
Why would it want to die
By jumping into a frying pan
And getting grilled or fried.

Must have a word with my great gran
I wouldn't jump into a frying pan.

Snow

Suresh bought a sledge
In the toy shop sale
"There's no flippin' snow"
He began to wail.

Spring passed by
And not a snow flake in sight
Poor Suresh
Couldn't sleep at night.

Summer came and went
Very hot and sticky
Finding snow
Was going to be extremely tricky.

Suresh moaned and groaned
"My sledge might have to go
If I don't find any flippin' snow."

Autumn rolled up
Crispy and bright
Not a hint of
A snow flake in sight.

Poor Suresh sank to a new low
As he glared out of the bedroom window
Mumbling and moaning "there's no flippin' snow."

December blew in
Dark and cold
Suresh shivered in bed
With just his teddy to hold.

Sleep wasn't easy as well you know
Suresh could only dream
Of sledging on snow.

Early next morning
Suresh shot out of bed
With a bit of a fright
He couldn't believe his room was so bright.

He pulled open the curtains
Then quickly let go
As he was confronted
By a street full of snow.

Zara's Zany Grandma

Zara's zany grandma Sandra
Owns a florist shop
Zara likes flower arranging
So she visits grandma quite a lot.

One sunny day whilst sorting flowers
Grandma shouted okay Zara stop
It's time we had a little treat
Let's go to the ice-cream shop.

Grandma Sandra shouted
What flavours have you got?
The daft ice- cream man said
Albatross smelly Trout and a new flavour called
Dead dogs eyes and snot.

Grandma Sandra smiled and mumbled
I could really eat the lot
I'm not greedy I will just have seventeen scoops
Of dead dogs eyes and snot.

Grandma grabbed her great big cornet
With seventeen scoops of dead dogs eye and snot
But didn't want sauce or sprinkles
Plonking on the top
She stuck a bunch of flowers in her ice-cream
Then scoffed the flippin lot.

Zara decided to have an ice-cream
She picked a flavour called Pigeons Pooh
Now she's covered in feathers
And walks around crowing coo coo coo coo coo.

What Have I Got?

Postman Pat's got a black and white cat.
Noddy's got a bell on his hat.

Andy Pandy's got Looby Loo.
Shaggy's got a dog called Scooby Doo.

Batman's got Robin - that's pretty cool.
Superman's got Lois Lane - he's no fool.

New York's got a lady with a torch in her hand.
Southport's got no ocean but loads of sand.

The Wooden Tops have a spotty dog.
Miss Piggy has a bright green frog.

The Chuckle Brother's are funny, funny, funny.
Winnie-the-Pooh has a big jar of honey.

Bill and Ben have a weed in a pot.
I'm just trying to think, what have I got?

Alice's Teddy

Alice claimed her Teddy could speak.
People said she was a bit of a freak.

Alice claimed he snored all night.
People groaned "She can't be right."

Alice said Teddy fell out of bed
He cried out loud as he banged his head.

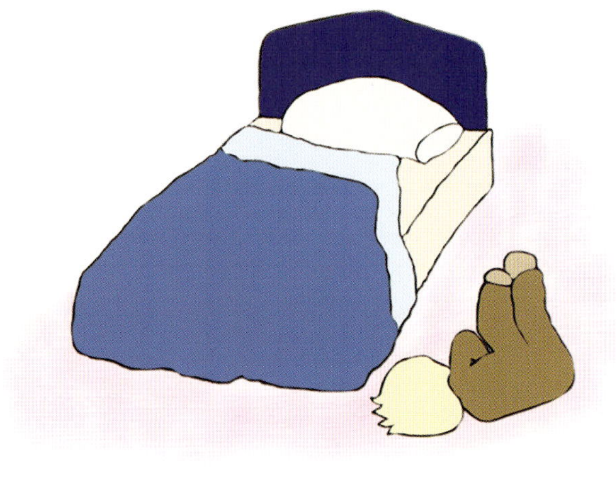

Nobody believed a word she said
But they'd never met her favourite Ted.

Every day in class at school
Alice was treated like the biggest fool.

When the school bell rang she was up and ready,
Shouting "Must get home! Must feed Teddy!"

Returning home, mother shouted "Dinner's ready!
Will you feed your baby brother, Teddy?"

Haunted House

Sometimes things go bump in the night
And you wake up in a state of fright

Just as you start to nod off again
You hear rattling and scratching on the window pane

Should get some sleep it's nearly four
Suddenly a great big crash on the garden shed door

Cats cry and dogs howl outside
They have no shelter or anywhere to hide

Scary shadows on my bedroom wall
Some are small some are tall
The scary shadows on my bedroom wall

Seven in the morning and it's getting light
That was a really frightening night

I'm not a wimp and I'm not a mouse
But this really is a HAUNTED house

“Get up dear Flavia” shouted mother it's nearly eight
Thought i heard rattling on the garden gate

“It”s just the milkman” claimed mother as she turned on the light
That was a very WINDY STORMY night.

Uncle Peter

My friend said her uncle Peter does not wash his hair
She also said....infact he does not really care
I said he must have nits
Or some kind of lice
My friend replied that i was nasty
That's not very nice
She claimed if her uncle heard me
He would be appalled
But she had not told me
That her uncle Peter is completely and utterly bald.

Twinkle Hill

Twinkle Hill was always ill
She hardly ever went to school
But Twinkle's mother had a plan
She wasn't anybody's fool.

Twinkle's mother has a friend at work
From a land far, far away
I know she said
"I will ring him up today."

Later that day
There was a loud knock on the door
Twinkle Hill just grunted
At the sight that she saw.

There was this great big man
Standing there
With knitting needles
Through his hair.

Twinkle gulped and shouted
"Flippin heck"
When she saw a necklace of chicken bones
Wrapped around his neck.

Mother said, "Darling just listen to me
This is my good friend Doctor Monkiwee
He's come all the way
From the mysterious Timbuckthree."

Doctor Monkiwee took one look and uttered
"This girl is velly, velly ill"
It could be the end
Of little Twinkle Hill.

Twinkle looked sad and whispered
"Please Doctor Monkiwee
Is there any chance
That you just might save me?"

"Well I have some pills made from the bark
Off the magical Ruby Tree
I brought them all the way
From my country Timbuckthree."

Mother was in the kitchen
Pouring a tube of Smarties onto a tray
She took the pink ones off
Then put rest away.

Mother put the smarties in a little bottle
Then shouted Doctor Monkiwee
"Here's those Ruby Tree tablets
You brought from Timbuckthree."

"Here you go little Twinkle Hill
Take these pills right away
Maybe there's a chance
Your illness will go away."

Next Morning Twinkle was up very early
Dancing up and down like a circus fool
Shouting, 'Mummy, Mummy Mummy
Please take me to school.'

I Really Don't Want To Go To School

Susan came down for her breakfast
Her jaw almost on the floor.
Her Mother spotted this
As she walked through the kitchen door.

"Mother dear," said Susan.
"Please don't think I'm a fool
But I really, really, really
Do not want to go to school."

"Give over Susan you'll be fine
As soon as you get there.
Now, come over here to me
And let me brush your hair."

Susan stared into the mirror,
"Do you think I'm a fool?
Because I really, really, truly
Do not want to go to school."

"Time to go!" said Susan's mother
With a little sigh.
"I've packed your lunch box
And given you an extra apple pie."

"Please don't make me go, mum.
And don't think that I'm a fool.
But I really, very seriously
Do not want to go to school."

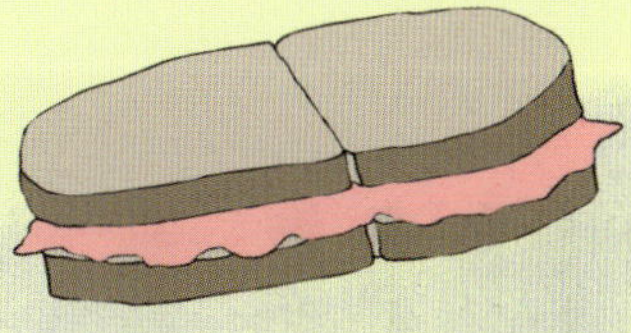

"Listen, darling daughter,
I don't mean to be a preacher,
But you have to go to school,
Because you're the flippin' teacher!"

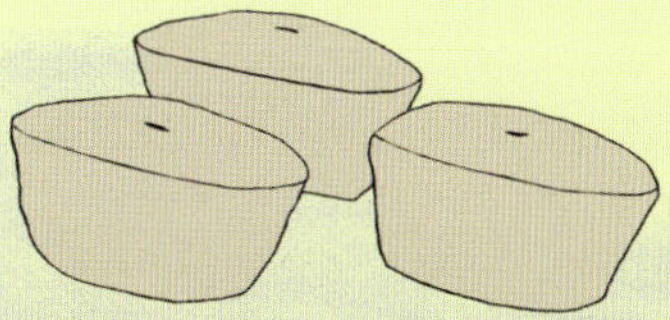

Smelly Cats and Dogs

Andrew Winston Crumps
Has a dog that does smelly trumps.
"Pooh," shouted Mr McGrew,
"Is that smell you young Andrew?"

Andrew's friend Simon Platt
Has a strange large cat
That leaves smelly presents
On Mr McGrew's front door mat.

Mr McGrew spotted Simon and shouted,
"Come here young Simon Platt
I want a word with you
About your strange smelly cat!"

Simon shot off sharply
To meet his friend Andrew
But he was closely followed
By a growling Mr McGrew.

Both boys hid
Hoping not to be seen
But Mr McGrew's eyes
Were very, very keen.

Mr McGrew caught them up
Near the corner shop.
"Oh no!" they screamed;
"Now we've had our lot."

Mr McGrew glared and said,
"Now I've caught up with you,
It's time we had a little chat
About smelly, smelly poo."

Mr McGrew smiled and whispered,
"We can solve this problem in a hurry.
Stop feeding your cat and dog
Peas, beans and curry."

Kitchen Capers

Kevin the kettle
Likes to blow off steam

Sally the scoop
Loves ice-cream

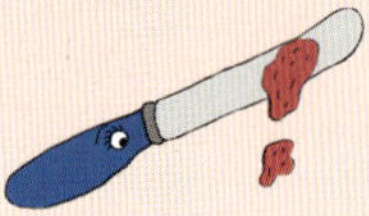

Katie the knife
Loves to spread strawberry jam

Eric the egg
Wants a frying pan

Stephen the soup bowl
Wants some broth

Christine the coffee pot
Loves to bubble and froth

Freya the fork
Wants to whisk some eggs

Willy the washing machine
Would like some new clothes pegs

Ella the egg timer
Doesn't need a clock

Wai's vegetables
Need a wok

Ollie the oven
Would like some bread to bake

Polly the plate
Wants a large slice of cake

Debbie the dish
Is keen on apple pie

Peeling onions
Can make you cry

Don't forget re-cycling
Shouted Robert the roasting tin

I'm over here
Bellowed the bright red bin

In went the spud peelings
Crumbs and old newspapers

Hope you clean up
After your kitchen capers.

Fishy Phone

Ringtone Johnny Jones,
Simply loves mobile phones.

He rings his Gran and his friends from school.
He plays tricky games he's no fool.

Now Friday night is Chippy tea.
Dad shouted, "Johnny, do you fancy joining me?"

Johnny answered, "Yes, and grabbed his mobile phone."
His dad said, "You should have left that phone at home."

Johnny banged his shoulder on the side of the chip shop door.
Then tripped over the mat, and landed on the floor.

Johnny's phone flew out of his hand climbing higher and higher.
Everybody thought it landed in the deep fat fryer.

Dad shouted, "We will buy a new one it doesn't really matter."
Nobody realised it had landed in the batter.

Dad placed the order three portions of fish, chips and peas.
Johnny smiled and whispered, "Dad you didn't say please."

Ringtones Johnny liked his food in a dish.
He set about cutting through the batter of his fish.

When suddenly, he let out a great big moan,
As he cut through the batter he saw his mobile phone.

Nothing Works

Haroon the helicopter could not fly
Zena the zebra only had one eye

Felix the fire engine did not have a bell
Leo the lion couldn't smell

Polly the police car has a broken flashing light
Olive the owl can't see at night

Tommy the tractor could not plough a field
The roman soldier didn't have a shield

Richard the rolls royce has a steering wheel that is stuck
So I tried a ford fiesta, still no luck

This is getting serious it's not a joke
Everything here is flippin broke

We even have a speed boat but we don't have a lake
We also have a racing car that has not got a brake

I've had enough I want to scream and shout
This is my very last time on this broken roundabout.

Wrong Day

Rudolph the blue nosed reindeer
Met father Easter on Boxing day
Father Easter scratched his head
As he had no toys on his sleigh

A little elf turned up shouting
No way no way no way
Wrong nose wrong father no toys
And the wrong flippin day.

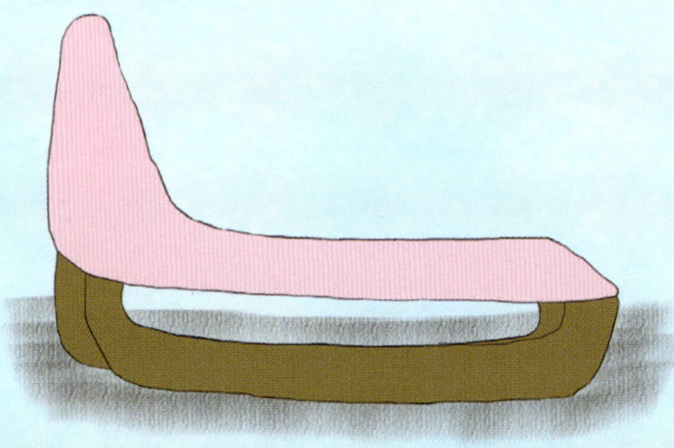

Ted

"Ted's dead!" said Fred.
"Ted's dead?" said Ned.
"Yes!" said Fred. "Ted's dead!"

"How did Ted become dead?" said Ned to Fred.
"He banged his head on the end of the bed.
Poor Ted." said Fred.

"Well," said Ned. "Poor Ted's dead."
Shame for Fred, he's lost poor Ted.

"Well," said Ned to Fred.
"What will you do now Ted's dead?"
"Simple." said Fred. "Ted's dead,
So I'll go the toy shop and buy a new one."

Pretty Little Tree

Poor little me, I'm just a pretty little tree.
I sit here in the breeze; I'm the nicest of the trees.

For the scorching sun I am made.
As I provide the people with dappled shade.

So why do people treat me bad?
It makes me angry, it makes me sad.

A snotty little boy carved his name on me,
And I just want to be a pretty little tree.

Lots of bird's poo on my leaves.
Just don't do it and I won't say please.

A scruffy little dog with a face like a skunk,
Cocked its leg and wee'd up my trunk.

Please, please, please think of me.
I just want to be a pretty little tree.

Mucky Maurice

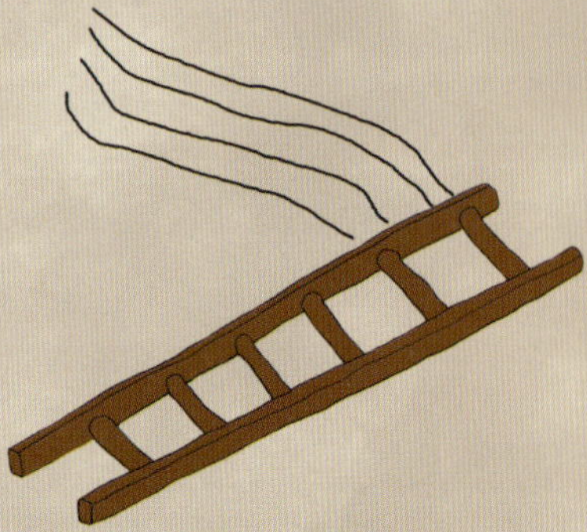

Mucky Maurice is a bit of a lad
Some say he's crazy
Some say he's mad
He finds trouble seven days a week
But poor old Maurice
He's really mild and meek

He trudged down a street
But tripped on the kerb
When suddenly a loud scream could be heard
He knocked the window cleaner off his ladder
Whose face turned purple,
As he raged madder and madder?

Maurice looked back as though nothing was wrong
He thought it was time to burst into song
"My name is Maurice
And I walk all day
Keeping trouble makers at bay"

Maurice breezed in to the superstore
He spotted boxes of cornflakes
Stacked up on the floor
A mountain of cornflakes
From the floor to the roof
Mucky Maurice needed some proof

Were they empty?
Or were they full?
Maurice grabbed a box and decided to pull
Crash, Bang, Wallop
Cornflakes everywhere
Maurice walked off not turning a hair

Adults pulled a face
Some started to moan
But the children shouted, "Just leave him alone"
We all love Maurice he's a real topper
And is also our local copper

Maurice smiled and broadly
He could do no wrong
Maurice walked off singing his favourite song
"My name is Maurice
And I walk all day
Keeping trouble makers at bay."

Trumping Great Gran

My great gran trumped
In the doctors waiting room
People glared at us both
With faces of gloom

Then she trumped
In the superstore
People glared more and more

She then let rip
In the cinema queue
People growled
Pooh pooh pooh

On the way home
She trumped on the bus
Everybody glared
At the pair of us

As we returned home
Great gran let a smelly one go
Dad glared at me
Grunting no no no.

Simon Slugbreath's Cat

Simon Slugbreath has a sneaky black cat
On his chest he had a little patch of white

He sleeps all day
Then creeps out late at night

He inches his way down the street
Past the old school house

Searching for a bird's nest
But he'd settle for a mouse

He knows every house that has a cat flap
He helps himself too other cat's food

Then saunters off into the night
He's very very rude.

Mr Turner and the Bunsen Burner

We learn a subject called science
At my new school

There's loads of apparatus
Which is pretty cool

Our teacher looks a little bit weird
He has curly hair, bushy eyebrows and a long brown beard

But yesterday disaster struck
Our poor science teacher didn't have much luck

Poor old Mr Turner
Ignited the Bunsen burner

His big bushy beard set alight
Which actually gave us all a fright

Flames shot up his beard higher and higher
His face lit up like a big bonfire

Suddenly his bushy eyebrows burst into flames
As well the curly mop of hair on top of his head

He was rushed off to hospital
Hope he's not dead.

Lucky Lucy Locket

Lucky Lucy Locket found a ticket in her pocket.
"There's a ticket in my pocket!" cried Lucky Lucy Locket.

Mother smiled as she brushed Lucy's hair.
"We bought a raffle ticket at the County Fair."

Two days later there was a knock on their front door.
As the man spoke, Mother's jaw nearly hit the floor.

Mother turned to Lucy "I have a surprise!
The ticket in your pocket has won first prize!"

"What have I won? A toy lamb that bleats 'bah bah'?"
"No! You've won tickets to see Lady Gaga!"

Lucy screeching dashed to Mother just like a NASA rocket,
"The ticket in my pocket makes me Lucky Lucy Locket!"

Mary's Plot

Mary had a little lamb
Who tried to steal her dinner.
Mary had a brain wave
I think I'm on a winner.

Mary disliked swede peas and turnips
And dreaded brussels sprouts
But every evening she would hear
"I've put your dinner out!"

"Come on Mary, eat your veg
They'll make you big and strong."
"That might be true, mum." Mary said
"But they make you trump and pong!"

Mary pushed her greens away
To one side of her plate,
Then smiled broadly as she saw
Her lamb walk through the gate.

It didn't take too long
Before the lamb greedily ate the lot
"Get out quickly!" Mary said,
"Before Mother spots my plot."

'Just in time' thought Mary
As her mum came through the door.
"Well done, my little girl," she said,
"And look! I've brought some more!"

Re-cycling

Wendy, Sharma and Michael
Thought it would be great to re-cycle

They collected bottles, cardboard and empty tins
Then placed them in the appropriate bins

Collecting for weeks they did really well
It made them happy.... everyone could tell

One day at the re-cycling centre the GIGANTIC truck arrived
They glared open mouthed, and eyes opened wide

Michael watched the tins,that were flattened then crushed
Followed by the bottles that were crushed into dust

Next was the cardboard chomped, chopped and pulped
Michael's mind wondered, as he licked his lips then gulped

Anything can be re-cycled in this enormous van
Michael had plans for his nasty old Gran.

Peter Jackson's Friend

Peter Jackson's friend was never rude.
Peter Jackson's friend did not eat food.

Peter Jackson's friend never made a noise.
Peter Jackson's friend never played with toys.

Peter Jackson's friend couldn't walk.
Peter Jackson's friend loved to talk.

Peter Jackson's friend didn't have a mum or a dad.
Peter Jackson's friend was never sad.

Peter Jackson's friend never shed a tear.
Peter Jackson's friend had no fear.

Peter Jackson's friend never had a drink.
Peter Jackson's friend didn't need to think.

Peter Jackson's friend wasn't a fool.
Peter Jackson's friend never went to school.

Peter Jackson's friend was a star on stage.
Peter Jackson's friend was all the rage.

Peter Jackson's friend was very funny.
Peter Jackson's friend is a ventriloquist dummy.

Don't Look Up

One lovely summer morning
I glanced up at the beautiful pastel blue sky
When an elegant Heron flew majestically by
Suddenly the dirty rotten smelly thing pooed
And it landed in my eye.